Everything You Need to Know About

SELF-
MUTILATION

A Helping Book
for Teens
Who Hurt Themselves

ASTOR HOME FOR CHILDREN

6___   ___ 5005
P____   ___ NY 12572

You don't need to hurt yourself. You can find more effective ways to cope with your problems.

• THE NEED TO KNOW LIBRARY •

Everything You Need to Know About

SELF-MUTILATION

A Helping Book for Teens Who Hurt Themselves

Gina Ng

THE ROSEN PUBLISHING GROUP, INC.
NEW YORK

For Glenn and my Mom, Dad, and Richard and the Gaerlan family.

Published in 1998 by The Rosen Publishing Group, Inc.
29 East 21st Street, New York, NY 10010

First Edition
Copyright © 1998 by The Rosen Publishing Group, Inc.

All rights reserved. No part of this book may be reproduced in any form without permission in writing from the publisher, except by a reviewer.

Library of Congress Cataloging-in-Publication Data

Ng, Gina.
    Everything you need to know about self-mutilation : a helping book for teens who hurt themselves / Gina Ng.
      p. cm. — (The need to know library)
      Includes bibliographical references (p.) and index.
      ISBN 0-8239-2758-X (lib. bdg.)
      1. Self-mutilation. 2. Teenagers—Mental health. 3. Adolescent psychology.
4. Stress in adolescence. I. Title. II. Series.
RJ506.S44N4 1998
616.85'82'00835—dc21
                                           98-20115
                                             CIP
                                             AC

Manufactured in the United States of America

Contents

Introduction

*J*odie slammed shut the door to her room, but she still could hear her mom yelling. "Don't you dare ignore me, young lady!" she screamed.

Tears streamed down Jodie's face. She knew her mom would continue yelling, but she would eventually pass out. Jodie knew she would have to go downstairs and face the mess her mom usually made when she drank. It's not fair, Jodie cried to herself, why can't she just stop drinking and behave like a normal mother?

Jodie slowly walked to her desk and took out a razor blade that was carefully hidden in the back of her drawer. She brought the blade to her upper arm and made a cut across the fleshy part of her arm. As Jodie watched the blood ooze from her wound, her tears stopped. A feeling of relief came over her.

Jodie cut herself a few more times before she felt strong enough to go downstairs and face her mother and her life.

Jodie is one of many teenagers who try to cope with their problems and difficulties by harming themselves. Some, like Jodie, cut themselves. Others may harm themselves by burning their skin, pulling their hair out from its roots, or banging themselves on hard objects until they break a bone or injure themselves.

These behaviors are known as self-mutilation, and for many teens they are a growing problem. It may be hard for some people to understand the extreme steps that certain teens take to cope with their difficulties. In a society where most people fear or try to avoid physical pain, why would anyone deliberately inflict pain upon themselves?

Many people may look down on self-injurers or mistakenly believe that self-injurers are "crazy" or "weird." These beliefs often are caused by fear, disgust, and ignorance of the problem. The reasons for this behavior are complex and sometimes difficult to understand. But people who hurt themselves have an illness, and they need support and understanding.

In this book, you will learn what self-mutilation is and why people harm themselves. You will also discover what symptoms to recognize if you are concerned about a friend or if you think you may be mutilating yourself. Finally, you will find out where to seek help.

People who harm themselves often do it secretly. They may feel isolated and alone. Teens who mutilate themselves need to know that there is help out there and that they are not alone. This book will aid teens in coping with their problems in a healthier and safer way.

Teenagers today face many problems and stressful situations.
They often feel as though they are isolated and alone.

Chapter 1

What Is Self-Mutilation?

"*I was flipping through a magazine the other day and saw an article about girls who were cutting themselves. I almost lost it, because recently I started cutting myself. I don't even know why I did it. I just had a big fight with my boyfriend, so I grabbed a razor and cut my wrist. I didn't really hurt myself that badly, but ever since then, whenever I have problems, I cut myself. After I read the article about those girls and how badly they hurt themselves, I knew I had to stop. I didn't want to end up like them. Their stories gave me the strength to confront my problems instead of hiding from them.*"

Self-mutilation is known by many names, including self-injury, self-harm, and self-abuse. Self-mutilation is not a new phenomenon. Religious ceremonies in countries around the world have included the practice for many years. But today some people are mutilating themselves secretly as a way to try to cope with their problems. Only recently have people begun to pay attention to and try to understand this disorder. Many doctors finally are able to properly diagnose it.

Self-mutilation is defined by experts as the act of intentionally harming one's body for emotional relief. These injuries are often severe enough to cause tissue damage. Although some think that people who self-mutilate their bodies actually are attempting suicide, self-mutilators do not want to kill themselves. When deaths occur involving self-injurers, they are often accidents. Death often results because the person has cut into an artery accidentally.

Self-injurers often cannot control their urges to hurt themselves. In the beginning, the behavior is their way of dealing with problems. Eventually it becomes their only way to cope. Many are unable to stop their self-mutilating behavior on their own.

According to Dr. Armando Favazza, a professor of psychiatry at the University of Missouri–Columbia's medical school and author of *Bodies Under Siege*, there may be as many as 2 million people in the United States alone who suffer from this illness.

In the teenage years, it is very common to see self-mutilation in both boys and girls. However, by the time they reach adulthood, female self-mutilators far outnumber male ones. For this reason, studies about self-mutilation have focused more on females than on males.

Self-mutilation has been practiced throughout the world for hundreds of years. It is part of initiation rites and tribal rituals in many cultures.

A 1989 survey involving 240 females in the United States (the only large-scale survey ever taken of self-mutilators) found that the average self-injurer starts at age fourteen. The survey also discovered that this self-injurious behavior often continues until the person reaches her late twenties or early thirties. The injuries inflicted often increase in severity during these years. The study found that the average self-injurer also suffers from eating disorders or has problems with alcohol or drugs.

The History of Self-Mutilation

As you learned earlier, self-mutilation has been practiced for hundreds of years in many different countries. Many rites of passage, initiation rites, and religious ceremonies include some form of self-mutilation.

Males from thirteenth- and fourteenth-century Christian cults and Australian Aborigines sliced open their penises along the urethra as a part of rites of passage. This act represented physical courage and served to bond together members of the same groups.

The Chinese practiced foot binding for thousands of years. Foot binding involved the mutilation of a woman's feet. The Chinese considered small feet to be a symbol of beauty and a sign of belonging to the upper class. A female's feet were bound in early childhood. A thick bandage was used to tightly wrap each foot, sparing only the big toe. Every few weeks, the bandage would be tightened. The goal was to break many of the bones in the foot, forcing the toes to bend into the sole. The government of China eventually outlawed this practice. Today foot binding is extremely rare. However, for many years some women still chose to have their feet bound.

In some parts of Africa, when tribal members meet during the New Year festival to resolve issues, members may mutilate themselves while in a trance. Although the wounds are sometimes severe, they often heal without complications. The self-mutilation symbolizes the healing within the community.

Fakir Musafar

Fakir Musafar is well known for body modification and mutilation. Some believe that he may be partly responsible for self-mutilation's growing popularity.

Musafar has been experimenting and working with self-mutilators for more than fifty years. At a very early age, he found himself wanting to change and hurt his body. His methods included binding his waist to nineteen inches and using a needle and thread to sew parts of his body together. He did this in secret for thirty years before he made his behavior public.

It was Musafar who suggested the idea for *Modern Primitive*, a first-of-its-kind book that focused on individuals who practice body modification. According to Musafar, this book encouraged many young people to see acts of self-mutilation as a type of ritual. To these young people, self-mutilation can also make their bodies look more attractive.

Teens who hurt themselves are not proud of their actions. They often do it to release intense emotional pain.

Today, Musafar is a certified director for a San Francisco state-licensed school for branding and body piercing. He now performs his rituals of body modification in public. One of these rituals, called O-Kee-Pa, involves Musafar hanging himself in the air, suspended by two giant hooks piercing his back.

For Musafar, self-mutilation is an art. However, many self-mutilators do not believe that they are making their bodies artistically attractive. They know that they are damaging themselves. They are not proud of their actions, as Musafar is. They are usually ashamed and embarrassed by what they do. These self-mutilators keep their behavior a secret. They use it as a way to deal with their emotional pain.

Types of Self-Mutilation

There are three different types of self-mutilation. The first type, major self-injury, is rare and very extreme. This form of self-injury results in the greatest harm done to the body. It includes castration or the amputation of a limb.

The second form is called stereotypic self-injury. This usually involves banging the head repeatedly on a hard surface, eyeball pressing, and finger and arm biting. This behavior is commonly seen in mentally challenged patients in institutions. It also occurs frequently in people suffering from disorders such as autism, schizophrenia, and Tourette's syndrome.

The third form of self-mutilation is called superficial, or moderate, self-injury. Moderate self-injury is the most common form of self-mutilation. It includes cutting, burning, skin picking, hair pulling (from the head and the body), bone breaking, and numerous other methods used to inflict "moderate" injuries on the body. The extent of the injuries can worsen over time. They may reach a point at which the person risks permanent disfigurement or accidental death.

"I guess I first started doing this because of my old man," says fourteen-year-old Daniel. "It was the same old routine. He came home from work and started drinking. By dinnertime, he was wasted. My mom accidentally burned his dinner, and he went crazy. He started slapping her. I just couldn't take it anymore. I tried to

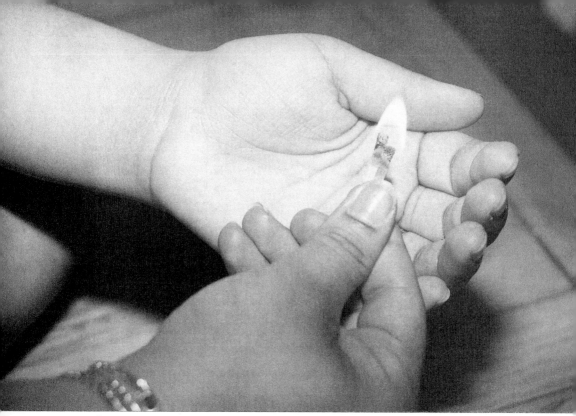

One way people may hurt themselves is by burning their skin with a candle or a match.

stop him and ended up with a busted lip and nose and a black eye. I was so frustrated and angry. I felt like I had this pressure building inside of me that I had to let out or I would explode. I started punching the wall.

"After about twenty minutes, my hands were raw and bleeding, but the pressure was gone. I didn't even feel any pain. All I felt was relief. After that, whenever I felt frustrated, I just banged myself on that wall. Sometimes I would punch it, kick it, or just slam against it until I felt better, or until I broke a bone."

Methods Used by Self-Injurers

Most people use a variety of methods to inflict superficial, or moderate, injuries upon themselves. According to a study conducted in 1989 by Karen Conterio and Dr. Favazza, the most common types of self-injuring methods are as follows:

- Cutting: 72 percent
- Burning: 35 percent
- Self-hitting: 30 percent
- Interfering with the body's healing process: 22 percent
- Hair pulling: 10 percent
- Bone breaking: 8 percent
- Multiple methods (combination of the above methods): 78 percent

Cutting

Cutting is the most popular self-injuring method. Injuries are most often inflicted on the wrists, upper arms, and inner thighs. Knives, razor blades, broken glass, and scissors are some of the instruments self-mutilators use to inflict injury. Some cutters slash themselves with broad, shallow strokes to inflict multiple wounds. Others cut themselves only once or twice, but the cuts are often deep and inflict greater pain and damage. Some self-mutilators even insert objects into their wounds, such as pins, glass, or nails.

Burning

Other self-mutilators harm themselves by burning their skin using fire or heat. Some burn themselves with fire, using matches, candles, or other sources.

Others heat metal instruments, such as frying pans, forks, and knives, over fire. They then press the hot metal directly onto their skin.

Self-Hitting

Someone who practices self-hitting uses his or her hands, arms, and legs to hit, punch, or kick himself or herself. Some self-injurers may use an instrument, such as a hammer, to hit themselves.

Interfering with the Body's Healing Process

These self-injurers pick at their wounds or scabs to prevent their body's healing processes.

Hair Pulling

Hair pulling is known as trichitillomania. This method of self-mutilation involves the pulling or plucking of hair from the scalp, eyebrows, eyelashes, and body. Males with facial hair also may pull at it. Hair pullers often pull out their hair and create a pile of hair before throwing it away.

Some self-mutilators pull out hundreds of strands of hair at one sitting. Others pull out only a few at a time but repeat this pattern throughout the day. Some even eat the hair.

Bone Breaking

Some self-injurers try to break their bones. They may run into walls or other hard surfaces repeatedly until a

Branding, piercing, and tattooing are not self-mutilation. People who mutilate themselves are often ashamed of their behavior and keep it a secret, rather than showing it off.

bone breaks. They may also bang body parts, such as arms, legs, or wrists, on a hard surface until they break a bone.

Fashion or Self-Mutilation?

The growing awareness of self-mutilation comes at a time when body modification, such as tattooing and body piercing, is becoming popular. Body modification is especially frequent among teenagers.

Extreme body art is also becoming popular today. This form of body modification involves scarification and branding. Scarification occurs when a person cuts his or her skin using a scalpel. He or she then may prevent the body's healing process to enhance the scars. Some people do this by splashing rubbing alcohol on a fresh wound and setting it on fire. Others put cigar ash or ink into open wounds. Some pick at the scabs of wounds to prevent healing.

Branding involves heating metal that has been twisted into a design. A person heats the metal, sometimes to temperatures of up to 1,800 degrees. He or she presses it quickly and firmly onto the skin. This is very painful. The purpose of both scarification and branding is to create a decorative scar.

Scarification and branding are becoming more fashionable. An increasing number of people are choosing this method to express their individuality. For example, it is common in some fraternities in the United States for members to be branded. Fraternity members believe that branding creates a feeling of brotherhood.

Finally, although many people now consider tattooing acceptable and fashionable, it was once a taboo. Not very long only, most people with tattoos were on the fringes of society. Many were criminals, bikers, and gang members. Today, many people, from actors to sports figures to musicians, have tattoos.

The increasing popularity of these practices has led many people to wonder if there is a difference between self-mutilation and body art. Many people, both male and female, pierce their ears. Is that considered self-mutilation? After all, they are deliberately harming and altering their bodies. They are puncturing their ear-lobes, scarring their skin, and making permanent holes in their ears.

The main difference between self-mutilation and body art is a person's reasons for choosing to alter his or her body. People who mutilate themselves are usual-ly trying to make themselves feel better by hurting their bodies. They often do this secretly and are ashamed of their actions. Many people who get an occasional tattoo or brand do it to make a statement. They want to be unique and set apart from the mainstream. They often proudly show their scars to others, rather than hiding them or covering them.

Another important difference between body modifi-cation and self-mutilation is control. Most people with tattoos, brands, and piercings decide to alter their bod-ies. They make a conscious decision. Many think long and hard about getting a tattoo, piercing, or brand before deciding. However, people who hurt their bodies are often unable to control their urges. They have to cut or hurt themselves to cope with daily problems in their lives. Once they lose control of their behavior, these people then become self-mutilators.

Now that you know what self-mutilation is, you need to understand why people would want to hurt their own bodies. The next chapter will focus on the reasons why people hurt themselves.

Chapter 2

Why Do People Hurt Themselves?

It may be hard to imagine how some people can hurt themselves. Why would they do this? Unfortunately, there is not an easy answer to this question.

Self-Mutilation and the Teenage Years

During your teen years, you face many situations that may cause frustration and stress. You may be experiencing peer pressure from friends about how to dress, how to talk, and even whom to date. At home, your parents may be pressuring you to get better grades, or they may not give you the freedom that you want. On top of all that, you have to deal with your rapidly changing and maturing body.

You may be increasingly aware of your sexuality. Maybe you are thinking about sex, questioning your

The physical and emotional changes that occur during the teenage years may cause confusion, tension, and fear.

own sexual attractiveness, or noticing other sexually attractive people more often. All of these pressures can combine to make you feel out of control or panicked. These feelings are very common among teenagers. Experts believe these physical and emotional changes and pressures may be why most people start their self-injuring behavior during their teens. Some people experience more turmoil during their teen years than at any other time in their lives.

Are there some days when you feel as if you can't cope anymore? We have all had those days, but we get through them. You know that not every day will be so bad. Some of you may cry or work out your frustrations in other ways. But some teens are unable to release this frustration in a healthy way. For them, the problems never seem to end. The frustration and pressure inside them just build. The only way for self-injurers to relieve their emotions is by hurting themselves.

According to *Self-Mutilation: Theory, Research, and Treatment*, a book by Paul M. Rosen and Barent W. Walsh, there are four basic thoughts that a person will have before he or she begins to harm him- or herself.

• Self-mutilation is okay or acceptable;
• The human body is disgusting, and it should be punished;
• Bad feelings can be reduced through certain actions;
• Only drastic measures will let others know about my feelings.

People who begin to hurt themselves may not even be aware of these ideas. However, subconsciously they have accepted and believe in these four thoughts. They use these beliefs to justify their self-injurious behavior.

Abuse and Self-Mutilation

Experts believe that children who were abused are at greater risk for self-injurious behavior. Many teens who hurt themselves have a history of abuse in their families (although there are those who have no history of abuse in their lives and still self-mutilate). Most self-mutilators were abused as children. This abuse can be physical, mental, or sexual.

When a child is abused, he or she experiences many emotions. Anger, guilt, shame, and frustration are just some of these feelings. When a person experiences a situation with which the mind cannot deal, such as abuse, the body responds to protect itself. It does this by separating that traumatic experience from the conscious mind. This is called dissociation. The result is often a feeling of numbness or separateness from the body.

In an article in the *New York Times Magazine*, Lisa Cross, a psychotherapist in New Haven, Connecticut, said, "When you are abused, the natural thing to do is to take yourself out of your body. Your body becomes the bad part of you that's being punished."

This separation leads teens to believe their bodies are bad and deserve to be punished. They reenact this punishment and hurt themselves when they feel they have been bad. Some may begin to blame themselves. They may think, If I just get better grades, or if I just listen more, then maybe Mom wouldn't hit me or wouldn't say such horrible things to me. As a result, they may begin to punish themselves by hurting themselves physically and emotionally.

Trauma Reenactment Syndrome

According to Dusty Miller, author of *Women Who Hurt Themselves*, women who engage in self-injuring behavior may be suffering from trauma reenactment syndrome (TRS). Injuries that women inflict on themselves

People who do not know how to work out their anger and frustration may turn to self-mutilation to release stress.

represent something that happened to them in child-hood. This is often abuse—physical or sexual.

Dr. Louise J. Kaplan, author of *Female Perversions,* argues that a person who was abused as a child and begins to hurt himself is reenacting the abuse. When he inflicts pain on his body, he is playing all the roles in the abusive relationship. He becomes the abuser, the victim, and even the soothing presence that takes care of him afterward.

For many people, caring for wounds is an important part of self-mutilation. They spend a great deal of time and attention on their bodies after they have injured themselves. Often they tend to wounds carefully and lovingly. By taking such good care of themselves, they

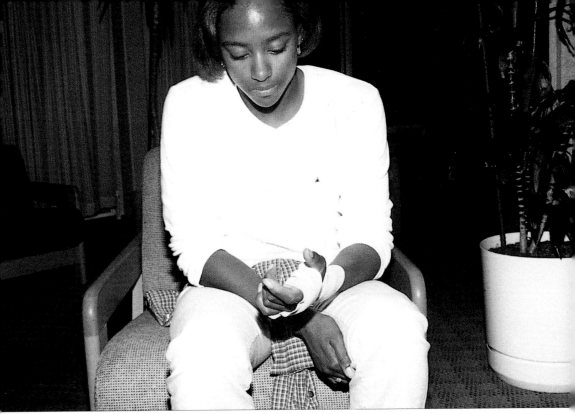

Some experts say that people who mutilate their bodies may be reacting to a traumatic event that occurred in their childhood.

are taking the place of the person who cared for them after they were abused in the past. Perhaps that caregiver was a parent, a sibling, or a close friend.

Miller believes that women begin to form a relationship with their self-injuring behavior. They become very protective about it and begin to rely upon it. She says, "The self-injurious behavior serves many functions: in a strange way, it serves both to keep others at a distance and to keep [the woman] from feeling alone. She experiences the behavior itself as a relationship. It may help her feel alive when she is overwhelmed by feelings of numbness. It can serve as well to keep her from feeling unbearable tension, rage, or grief. Her behavior is also a cry for help, a request for the protection she did not receive as a child."

Control

Many experts believe that power and control play important roles in why a person hurts himself. When a person is abused, especially sexually abused, he feels as if he has no control over his body. The abuser controls the body. In an effort to take back control, the person begins to hurt himself. One self-injurer, who was sexually abused when she was seven, claims, "If somebody else is hurting me or making me bleed, then I take that instrument away, and I make myself bleed. It says you can't hurt me anymore. I'm in charge of that."

According to Raelyn Gallina, a body artist who uses paper towels to take impressions of her blood designs, there is a symbolic experience to the scar. In the July 27, 1997, issue of the *New York Times Magazine*, she says, "You know that you're going to endure some pain, you're going to shed your blood. . . . That act, once it happens and you come out victorious, makes you go through a transformation. We have so little control over what goes on. . . . It comes down to you and your body."

Emotional Release

People who hurt themselves often hide their emotions rather than face them. They bury them deep inside as a way to cope with the stress their emotions cause. They go on with their lives as if everything is okay. In time, the emotions become a separate part of their bodies.

Because they have separated their bodies from their emotions, these people often feel numb or dead. They

For some teens, physical pain is the only way they can cope with their overwhelming emotions.

may hurt themselves to ensure that they are really still alive. Some self-injurers report that they feel alive only when they bleed.

For other people, self-injuring behavior becomes a way to release their emotions. They are substituting intense physical pain for emotional pain. They are reducing the level of their mental distress by experiencing physical distress. For them, physical pain is easier to handle than overwhelming emotions.

More Women Than Men Hurt Themselves

Statistics show that a higher percentage of women are treated for self-injuring behavior than men. According to Miller, this may be because many women think negatively about their bodies. Society places a lot of importance on a woman's body. The ideal woman should be tall, thin, and beautiful. For most women, these standards are impossible to reach.

Many women feel that they do not measure up to the women they see in movies, on television, and in magazines. They often believe that their worth as a person depends upon their bodies and their physical attractiveness. As a result, they begin to think that they are not valuable or important as people. For some of these women, their bodies become their enemies and the targets of their own violence.

Another reason that more women than men mutilate themselves may be because some parents teach their daughters that some emotions, such as anger, are not feminine and therefore are not appropriate to express. They are taught to hide their emotions because it is not polite or acceptable to show them. The only way they can release these emotions is by hurting their bodies.

Men and Violence

This is not to say that men do not hurt themselves. Statistics show that an equal number of boys and girls hurt themselves in their teenage years. However, that rate drops by the time boys reach adulthood.

Some experts believe that, because of the many pressures females face about their bodies, they tend to turn their negative emotions, such as anger, inward. They begin to hurt themselves and their bodies. Men, on the other hand, turn their anger outward to others. This may result in physical violence toward others. Perhaps this is why some men who have been victims of abuse during their childhood become violent adults.

Self-Injury and Addiction

Some experts believe that self-injury may be addictive. An addiction is a compulsive need to do something, even though it may harm you and others. A person with an addiction feels this need so strongly that he or she is willing to risk the dangerous or painful consequences of his or her actions. An addiction may destroy relationships with family and friends, hurt an addict's body and brain, and even result in death for some.

When a person who self-mutilates first hurts him- or herself, it relieves pressure. However, the self-injurer must hurt him- or herself more often and with increasingly serious wounds to get this same relief. This process is very similar to the way people become addicted to drugs or alcohol. At first, a little alcohol or drugs are enough to make them feel better. Gradually they need to increase their intake to get the same effect.

Some experts believe that self-mutilating releases hormones called beta-endorphins. In this way, self-mutilation is like an addiction. Beta-endorphins stop pain and make a person feel good. Some self-injurers have reported feeling high from their experiences. Others have described bleeding that leads to a sense of release or relief.

Self-mutilation is a complex disorder. There are many factors that trigger this reaction to stress. But when the body is injured, deliberately or otherwise, there are consequences. Self-mutilation can lead to permanent disfigurement, the loss of a limb, or even death. The next chapter will discuss these consequences.

Chapter 3

The Consequences of Self-Mutilation

*C*aitlin ran up to her father as he got out of his car. *"Dad, I think something's wrong with Janeece. She's been in the bathroom ever since I got home. She locked the door and won't answer me!" Caitlin cried.*

Caitlin's dad rushed to the bathroom. He called out to Janeece, but she didn't answer. "Honey, are you okay? Your sister and I are really worried. Open the door."

No sound was coming from inside the bathroom, and Caitlin's dad knew something was wrong. He rushed to find his toolbox. When he finally got the door to open, he and Caitlin saw Janeece lying in the middle of the bathroom floor. She was unconscious, surrounded by a pool of blood.

Caitlin and her dad rushed Janeece to the hospital, where the doctors worked hard to save her life. It was a close call, but they said that Janeece would live.

The doctors found numerous scars on Janeece's legs. Her parents also found a bloody razor in the bathroom. A doctor who specializes in self-mutilation cases told

Janeece's parents that she had been cutting her thighs with a razor. It appeared that she had cut too deeply and accidentally sliced open an artery.

When a person first starts hurting her body, it does not take much pain to give her emotional relief. Once she feels in control again, she can stop. But it is important to remember that self-mutilation is similar to addiction. Like an addict, the person gradually will need to inflict more severe injuries to feel that same level of relief. Also, as the behavior continues, she starts to lose control of it. Eventually, self-mutilation becomes a compulsion. The self-mutilator has to fight the urge not to hurt herself. As the severity of her injuries increases, so does the chance that she will do permanent and serious damage to her body.

For example, when a person first begins to cut herself, she may need to use only a few shallow cuts to feel relief. Later she may need to cut using deep strokes to feel better. These deep strokes increase the chance that she may cut into a vital body part, such as an artery, which can endanger her life.

Accidents

Most people who hurt themselves are only looking for a way to cope with their problems. They do not want to commit suicide. However, death can sometimes result. In some cases, people have died during a self-mutilation episode.

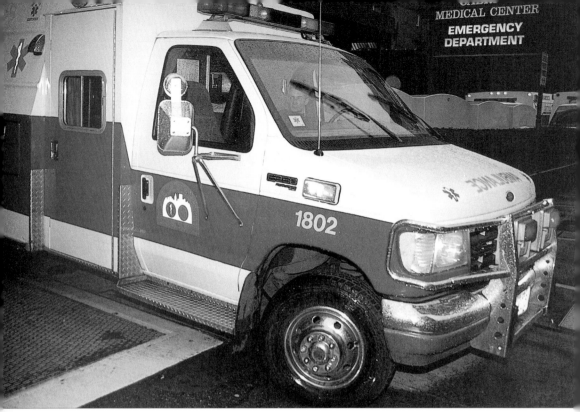

Sometimes self-mutilation can become so serious that it requires emergency care.

A person who cuts himself risks cutting too deeply. He can permanently sever tendons, arteries, and other body parts. His body may not heal properly, or it may not heal at all. He may lose full movement in his limbs if tendons are severed and do not heal. Finally, a cutter can bleed to death.

Someone who repeatedly bangs his body into hard surfaces, like a wall or a table, risks breaking a bone. If he bangs his head against something hard, he may suffer a concussion.

Someone who pulls out his hair and eats it risks forming hair balls in his stomach. These hair balls can cause nausea, vomiting, bleeding in the stomach, and other, more serious conditions.

Many of these conditions may require emergency care. Unfortunately, self-mutilators tend to hurt themselves secretly, usually behind locked doors. If they are unable to call for help, they will not get the medical attention that they need.

Drugs and Self-Mutilation

Self-mutilators also may be addicted to alcohol or drugs. People who injure themselves while under the influence of drugs and alcohol risk more severe injuries. Because people high on drugs or drunk are not in control of their actions, they may accidentally hurt themselves more severely than they intended. A shallow cut may easily become a very deep cut.

Drugs also alter users' senses and their perceptions of reality. Some drugs enable people to withstand extreme amounts of pain. Others cause them to see or hear things that are not really there. Because of this, self-mutilators may not realize how badly they are injured. They may not notice that they are even hurt at all. By the time self-mutilators realize that they need medical attention, it may be too late.

Infection

People who cut or burn themselves risk developing dangerous infections. The instruments they use to cut, such as razors, knives, and shards of glass, are not sterilized. A person faces the possibility of infection with any open wound. When the skin is broken, bacteria and germs can

People who use instruments to hurt themselves risk infection from the objects and open sores.

enter the body and cause an infection. Infections need to be treated with antibiotics. Left untreated, infections can have serious consequences, such as severe disfigurement or loss of the infected body part.

Burning the skin also causes dangerous infections. This is especially true if an object is used to burn the skin. When an object is heated up and pressed onto the skin, bits of the metal can be left on the skin. Taking out this metal can be a long and painful experience. Leaving it in can lead to serious infections.

Scars

According to statistics, most people who self-mutilate eventually grow out of this behavior. Sadly many of these people will have scars for the rest of their lives. These scars can be hurtful, emotionally and physically.

Friends, co-workers, and others may ask about the source of the scars. Explaining can be especially hard if the scars are severe or in unusual places. Meeting people, interviewing for jobs, wearing short sleeves or shorts, or going to the beach can be difficult. As adults, former self-mutilators may be emotionally stable and may have stopped self-mutilating. Yet questions from friends and stares from strangers may always serve as reminders of self-mutilators' past behavior. The scars may also bring back painful memories of very unhappy times in their lives.

Some people can have their scars removed surgically. Others take measures to hide them. Although plastic surgery, body lotions, and makeup can conceal scars, these methods are often bothersome or expensive.

Emotional Consequences

Self-mutilation greatly affects a person's emotions. A person who self-mutilates has unresolved emotional problems that she cannot handle. As long as she is self-mutilating to deal with her painful emotions, she is avoiding those feelings. Burying emotions can be psychologically harmful.

Everyone has problems from time to time, but most people face them. They learn to deal with their pain. Eventually they are able to admit and solve their problems and go on with their lives. It is when a person avoids these issues, through behaviors such as self-mutilation, that problems never go away.

It is never too late to learn better ways of dealing with your problems. You do not have to hurt your body in order to cope.

Chapter 4

Profiling Self-Injurers: Who Are They?

W ho are the people who hurt themselves? Why do they do it? In this chapter, we will look at some self-injurers, from average teenagers to famous celebrities.

Famous Self-Mutilators

Well known cutters include the late Princess Diana and actor Johnny Depp. In Andrew Morton's biography of Princess Diana, he revealed that Diana not only suffered from an eating disorder. She also had episodes of self-injuring behavior. Some of these behaviors included cutting her wrist with a razor, throwing herself against a glass cabinet, and cutting her chest and thighs.

In a May 1993 article in *Details* magazine, Johnny Depp talked about the self-inflicted scars on his forearm. He compared his body to a journal. He said he cut himself with a knife to mark the special times in his life.

Anyone can begin practicing dangerous self-mutilating behavior. The late Princess Diana had a history of self-mutilation.

These episodes of Princess Diana and Johnny Depp show that no one, no matter how famous or wealthy, is immune to this problem.

The Typical Self-Injurer

A typical self-injurer is female and in her mid-twenties to early thirties. Her behavior started in her teen years. She is white and middle or upper-middle class. She is well-educated and intelligent. The typical self-injurer also comes from a home where there was physical or sexual abuse or has lived with at least one alcoholic parent. She may suffer from an eating disorder too.

It is important to remember that this is only a profile of the average self-injurer. Many kinds of people mutilate themselves. They are male and female, from all ethnic groups, and from all social classes. They have different sorts of families. Just because someone does not fit into the typical profile does not mean that he is not a self-mutilator or is not at risk.

People who mutilate themselves often share similar experiences:

- Physical, emotional, or sexual abuse during childhood
- Parental alcoholism or abuse of other drugs by parents
- Neglect or abandonment by a parent
- Loss of a parent through death or divorce
- Tense or abusive relationship between parents

If someone you know is unable to cope with his emotions, dislikes his body, and is unable to express his feelings, he may be at risk for self-mutilating behavior.

Personality traits that self-mutilators commonly share include:

• Constant aim for perfection
• Dislike of one's body
• Inability to cope with strong emotions
• Inability to release or express emotions to others
• Frequent mood swings

Episodes of self-mutilation result from the following feelings:

• Anger
• Rejection

- Failure
- Loss or abandonment
- Helplessness

An average self-injurer always strives for two things: keeping the self-mutilation a secret and remaining in control of him- or herself.

"It's all mine," said one self-injurer about her behavior for an interview in the July 27, 1997, issue of the *New York Times Magazine*. "It's nothing that anybody can experience with me or take from me. I guess it's like my little secret. I've got physical scars. It shows that my life isn't easy. I can look at different scars and think, yeah, I know when that happened, so it tells a story. I'm afraid of them fading."

"After a really bad day, I sometimes feel so out of control. My parents, school, my boyfriend, who is always pressuring me to have sex. It seems like everyone else is trying to control my life, and I don't have a say in anything. I lock the door to my bedroom. I line my floor with towels so that my blood doesn't stain the carpet. I also have paper towels around in case I need to soak up extra blood. I take out a fresh razor blade and just cut. Sometimes I just slash, and other times I carve words on my body. When I see myself bleed, it's like all the confusion, the anger, just pour out along with the blood.

"Afterward, I feel such relief. It gives me back a feeling of control and strength to face all my problems. I

don't know anything else that could give me this feeling of relief."

These two anonymous teenagers are keeping their behavior a secret. They think they have everything under control. But do they? Hurting their bodies is not going to solve any of their problems.

Do You Know a Self-Mutilator?

If you think someone you know may be hurting herself, there are signs you can recognize. Self-injurers often act in the following ways:

• They have difficulty expressing or handling emotions;
• They have frequent unexplained injuries;
• They wear long pants and long-sleeved shirts regard-
   less of the weather;
• They isolate themselves from others.

Is a friend or family member showing these signs? If you feel that someone you know may be mutilating his or her body, it's important to encourage your friend to get help.

How to Help

   If you believe that someone you know is mutilating herself, there are things you can do to help her. She may come to you and admit her behavior on her own. Or you may have to approach her and tell her that you

If you know someone who is injuring herself, try to listen to her in a nonjudgmental, understanding manner.

know about her self-mutilating. Regardless, there a few
tips you should remember:

1. Maintain an accepting, open attitude about her self-
   mutilation. She may be ashamed and embarrassed
   by her behavior. Try to act nonjudgmental. You need
   to make her feel safe and secure discussing her problem with you.

2. Recognize the severity of the self-mutilator's problems and her intense pain. Also recognize that she is
   unable to stop hurting herself. Try not to get angry
   at her self-injuring behavior. If she could stop, she
   would. Acknowledge that she is under a lot of stress
   and offer to help in any way you can.

3. If you think she is in danger of seriously harming
   or even killing herself, stay with her until her urge
   to hurt herself passes. Encourage her not to be alone
   when she feels this way.

4. Encourage the self-mutilator to talk with an adult
   about her problem. Ideally, she should speak with a
   therapist about her self-mutilation. But a parent,
   teacher, guidance counselor, coach, or member of the
   clergy can help too.

5. Self-mutilation is an extremely difficult, stressful, and
   frustrating experience for everyone involved. When

you are trying to help a friend, you may be faced with many powerful emotions of your own. You cannot keep all these emotions to yourself. Find someone with whom you can talk and from whom you can get emotional support.

Chapter 5

Getting Help

If you are hurting yourself to deal with your problems, it is important that you get help fast. This chapter will discuss some healthy methods you can use to better cope with your problems. It will also tell you where you can get help.

If you feel like hurting yourself, it is important to ask why. Intense emotions often trigger self-mutilation. Ask yourself the following questions:

- Why do I want to hurt myself? What has happened that makes me want to do this?
- Is there something else I can do to make this feeling go away, other than hurting myself?
- What am I feeling now?
- How will I feel about myself if I go through with this urge? Will it solve my problem?
- Do I really need to hurt myself?
- Is there a way I can avoid the situation that makes me want to hurt myself in the future?

If you feel an urge to hurt yourself, try writing down your thoughts and feelings in a journal.

These questions may seem hard to ask and even harder to answer. However, they will become easier with time, as long as you truly want to find another way to solve your problems. It may be helpful to write your answers down. Anything you can do to keep yourself busy and delay your actions will increase your chances of not hurting yourself. Writing down your feelings also will enable you to better understand why you are hurting yourself.

"I recently admitted my self-mutilation to my best friend. She was shocked at first. She really didn't understand what it was, but I knew I had done the right thing because she didn't make any judgment, and she wasn't disgusted. That was my greatest fear. She accepted it, and she supported me. She listened to me talk about my problems at home and my feelings. I felt a sense of relief because I actually had someone to talk to. It was like the burden was lessened because I could share it.

"She suggested that I write my feelings in a journal. She said that helps her when she has a problem. So I tried it. Anytime I felt overwhelmed or I felt like hurting myself, I would pull out my journal and just write. It helps tremendously."

Distract Yourself

Think of some activities you can do to keep yourself busy when you feel the urge to hurt yourself. Call a friend. Occupy your mind with other things so that you won't think about hurting yourself. Go for a run or do some other physical activity, such as lifting weights or doing household chores. Physical activity can help to reduce stress and tension. It also releases endorphins, which are hormones that make the body feel good.

Lastly, try to do something you enjoy or something that makes you happy. Buy yourself a gift, treat yourself to a movie, or do something that calms you. People who hurt themselves tend to suffer from low self-esteem. They do not think they deserve to be happy. But you need to tell yourself that you are a good, smart, beautiful person. Don't judge yourself so harshly. No one is perfect, but everyone deserves to be happy.

If none of the above methods works, and you still feel the urge to hurt yourself, experts recommend that you try to distract yourself with some sort of minor pain. One method is to wear a rubber band around your wrist and snap yourself with it. Another is to substitute your usual self-mutilating action with something else. Instead of slashing yourself with a knife or other sharp object, use a red marker. These activities may bring you emotional release without harming your body.

Although these methods may be able to help you stop self-mutilating, it is still important that you tell someone about your problem.

"It was hard admitting that I needed help," thirteen-year-old Ray says. "I didn't want to tell anyone what I did. But it was becoming a problem. I got addicted to my

cutting. There were times when I almost couldn't control myself. It scared me a little that I couldn't stop. Although I knew I needed to tell someone if I was going to get help, I didn't know who could help me. I was afraid they would think I was a freak.

"I finally decided to tell my parents. They were shocked at first, but I think it got them to realize what their constant arguing was doing to me. They took me to see a doctor, and we all went to see a therapist. It got a lot better after that. I'm no longer cutting, and although I still get the urge from time to time, I know I can face my problems head-on."

Telling Family and Friends

Admitting your self-injurious behavior to your family and friends can be difficult. You may fear how they will react. You may be afraid they will reject you or jump to hasty conclusions.

When you decide to reveal your secret to someone, it is important to pick a place and time in which you will not be hurried or interrupted. Let the person know that, by admitting your behavior, you are showing that you trust and love him. Realize that this information may be difficult for someone you love to hear. Your admission may make him think that he has done something wrong.

Also, do not tell him in anger. Both sides need to come together to openly discuss the problems that cause you to self-mutilate. This is a time to communicate, not to exchange accusations.

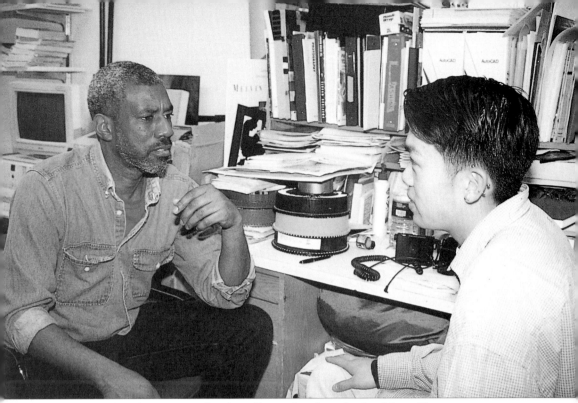

People who are professionally trained to deal with self-mutilating behavior can help you stop hurting yourself.

Seek Professional Help

The next important step is to seek professional help. You need to see someone who is specially trained to help people deal with emotional issues.

One of the most well known organizations that helps people with self-injuring behavior is the S.A.F.E. (Self-Abuse Finally Ends) Alternatives Program. The program, located in Illinois, was developed by Karen Conterio and Wendy Lader, Ph.D. Its goal is to help those suffering from self-injuring behavior. S.A.F.E. can help self-mutilators cope with the problems in their life. An experienced team of psychiatrists, psychologists, social workers, nurses, and mental health counselors work together to help patients. There is also a team of specialists who help deal with self-injurers' other problems, such as alcohol and drug abuse, eating disorders, abuse in a family, and other related issues.

The program accepts both teenagers (ages thirteen to eighteen) and adults. Although S.A.F.E. accepts both males and females, 99 percent of their patients are female. Also, patients who wish to enter the program must agree to sign a contract promising they will not hurt themselves.

Inpatient and Outpatient Programs

S.A.F.E. offers three programs: inpatient, outpatient, and the Day Hospital program. The outpatient program is for those whose conditions are stable and who are able to control their self-injuring behavior. These patients come to the program only for therapy sessions.

The inpatient program is for those who are in immediate danger of harming themselves permanently or who are hurting themselves severely. Often those who were unsuccessful in the outpatient program enter the inpatient program.

The Day Hospital program is for those whose cases are not appropriate for either the inpatient or the outpatient programs. Their conditions are not severe enough for the inpatient program. However, they are not ready for the outpatient program yet, either.

Patients usually stay in the program for thirty days, and housing is provided when necessary. Doctors at the program can extend this time period if they feel the patient's behavior warrants a longer stay. You can contact S.A.F.E. at (800) DONTCUT for more information.

Although S.A.F.E. is perhaps the best-known program for self-mutilators, it is far from the only one. Many communities are starting programs to help self-mutilators. Some of these offer therapy similar to S.A.F.E.'s; others are self-help groups. Talk to a guidance counselor, doctor, or mental health professional if you are having trouble finding a program in your area.

Although self-mutilation often ends on its own, it usually takes ten to fifteen years to do so. During this time, you can do serious damage to your body—physically and emotionally. If you engage in self-injuring behavior, it is important to seek help immediately.

It may be difficult to tell others about your behavior. However, there are specialists who understand this disorder, and they can help you to recover. You also can find support from your family and friends.

Self-mutilation is an unhealthy and dangerous way to cope with your problems. Don't hide from your problems or allow them to control your life. We all face problems in our lives, but each time we solve one, we become stronger. You can face your difficulties head-on and learn to deal with your problems in healthy ways.

Glossary

addiction A compulsive need to do something, even though it may harm you and others.

amputation When a body part, such as a leg or an arm, is cut off.

autism A disorder in which someone experiences repetitive movement and is unable to function in society.

beta-endorphins Hormones in the body responsible for making a person feel good and free from pain.

body modification Permanent changes made to the body.

branding Using hot metal to burn the skin to create a decorative scar.

castration The removal of the penis.

compulsive Being unable to control an action.

conscious To be aware or alert.

dissociation Separating one thing from another, such as putting an experience out of your mind.

enhance To heighten or increase.

fraternity A club or society made up of male members, usually found at a college.

inflict To give something harmful to someone.
mainstream Popular or common.
modification The act of changing something.
multiple Many or a multitude.
phenomenon An event or happening.
psychotherapist A person trained to help people deal with emotional problems.
reenact To re-create a situation.
rite of passage A ceremony that marks a person's movement from one stage of life to another.
ritual A formal ceremony.
scarification The creation of a design on the skin with scars.
schizophrenia Disorder in which someone has lost contact with reality.
sexuality The quality of being a sexual person or having a sexual identity.
sterilize To get rid of germs and bacteria.
taboo Forbidden or banned.
tattooing Using ink or dye to create permanent designs on the skin.
Tourette's syndrome A disease in which someone experiences uncontrollable movements, behaviors, or speech.
trichitillomania Disorder in which someone plucks body hair from the roots.
urethra A tube which, in males, runs from the bladder through the penis.

Where to Go for Help

The Cutting Edge
P.O. Box 20819
Cleveland, OH 44120
The Cutting Edge is a newsletter about self-injury.

Pittsburgh Action Against Rape
81 South 19th Street
Pittsburgh, PA 15203
(412) 431-5665
Web site: http://www.paar.ml.org

S.A.F.E. (Self-Abuse Finally Ends)
Alternatives Program
40 Timberline Drive
Lemont, IL 60439
Hotline: (800) DONTCUT
Web site: http://www.rockcreek-hosp.com
This phone number is a national information line that will give referrals to therapist-led support groups throughout the United States.

In Canada

S.A.F.E. in Canada
306-241 Simcoe Street
London, ON N6E 3L4
(519) 434-9473
Web site: http:///www.wwdc.com/safe/
e-mail: safe@wwdc.com
This organization is not affiliated with the S.A.F.E.
Alternatives Program in Illinois.

Web Sites

http://www.girlzone.org
A nonprofit organization dedicated to building girls'
self-esteem.

http://www.gurl.com
An on-line magazine for girls that deals with issues
such as body image, self-esteem, and sexuality.

http://www.mindspring.com/~thefly/selfinjury.htm
A self-injury support group.

http://www.palace.net/~llama/psych/injury.html
A self-injury support group.

For Further Reading

Bottsworth, Loralei, as told to Stephanie Pedersen. "Making the Cut." *Teen*. March 1998.

Egan, Jennifer. "The Thin Red Line." *New York Times Magazine*. July 27, 1997.

Miller, Dusty. *Women Who Hurt Themselves*. New York: Basic Books, 1994.

Reybold, Laura. *Everything You Need to Know About the Dangers of Tattooing and Body Piercing*. New York: The Rosen Publishing Group, 1996.

Wilkinson, Beth. *Coping with the Dangers of Tattooing, Body Piercing, and Branding*. New York: The Rosen Publishing Group, 1998.

Challenging Reading

Favazza, Armando R. *Bodies Under Siege*. Baltimore, MD: Johns Hopkins University Press, 1996.

Index

About The Author

Gina Ng is an editor and freelance writer living in New York City.

Photo Credits

Photo on page p. 11 by Charles & Josette Lenars/Corbis; p. 19 by Reuters/Steve
Dipaola/Archive Photos; p. 30 by Ira Fox; p. 42 by Huton-Deutsch
Collection/Corbis; p. 44 by Maike Schulz. All other photos by Brian Silak.

ASTOR HOME FOR CHILDREN
PROFESSIONAL LIBRARY
6339 MILL ST PO 605
RHINEBECK, NY 12572